This book belongs to

_____

Sydney the Monster Stops Cyber Bullies

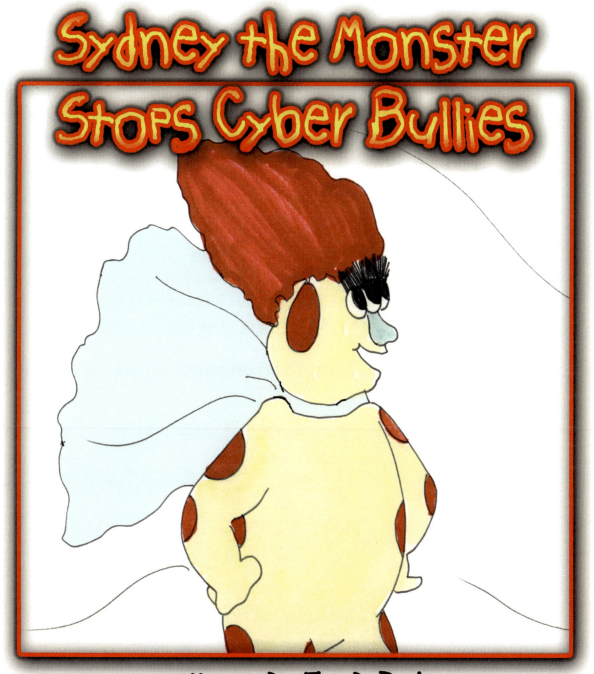

written by Dr. Tom DePaoli
illustrated by Laurie Barrows

This book or parts thereof may not be reproduced in any form, stored in a retrieval system, or transmitted in any form by any means- electronic, mechanical, photocopy, recording, digital, or otherwise-without prior written permission of the author and illustrator, except as provided by United States of America copyright law.

Text © Dr. Tom DePaoli
www.apollosolutions.us

Illustration & Book Design ©2017 Laurie Barrows
"Making the World a Happier Place, One Smile at a Time" ™

www.LaurieBarrows.com

ISBN-13: 978-1544921655
ISBN-10: 1544921659

Printed in the United States of America

Published in the United States of America

Dedication

This book is dedicated to all children, parents, relatives, and teachers who stand up to cyber bullies.

learning

puzzled

peaceful

serious

surprised

thinking

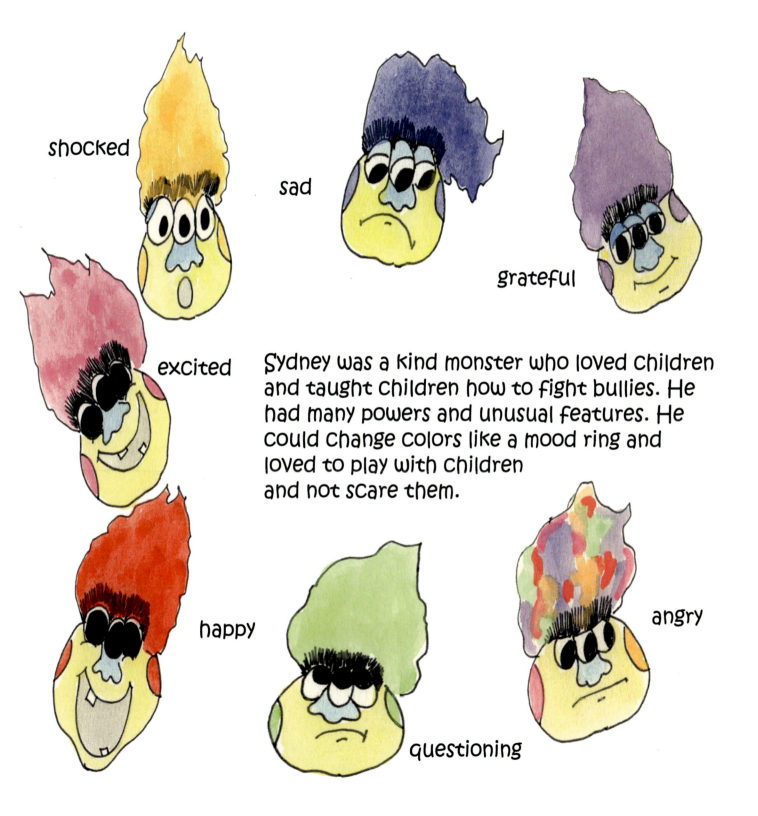

Sydney was also a skilled computer geek who loved to design computer games for children.

One day Sydney saw a child with her head down and crying at her computer desk. Sydney asked what was wrong.

The girl said, "Someone has been posting awful things about me on the Internet." She showed Sydney some of the postings

Sydney was shocked at the nastiness of the postings and he decided he had to help her.

First Sydney he searched for the definition of cyber bullying. He found this:

Cyberbullying can include threats, insults, slurs, bashing or infecting the victim's computer with a virus or slowing it down. The behavior must be deliberate, repeated often, intended to cause harm and can be on any electronic device including cell phones, computers, tablets etc.

Sydney sat down at the computer and went right to work. He found a list of general actions that a child and parents can do to prevent cyberbullying and showed it to the girl.

Anti-Cyber Bullying Actions

- First understand and research what cyberbullying is and is not.
- Keep strong passwords and always protect your private information.
- Make sure all photos are appropriate and not compromising.
- Never open email that you do not recognize.
- Never leave an account logged in…always log out.
- Stop and do not respond to any provocative posts, emails or text messages. Cool off awhile. Do not retaliate.
- Join groups and raise awareness of cyberbullying.
- Make sure your privacy controls on your accounts are at the maximum-security level.
- Check online information about yourself on Google and other websites.
- Treat others with respect online and do not become a cyberbully.

Then Sydney immediately went to each of the websites and filed a harassment report with the site.

He formally asked the webmaster to delete the posts immediately.

He made double sure that all the websites were addressed.

Sydney knew that he had to do some more actions. He called a meeting of parents and teachers and let them know about the cyber bullying what had happened. He first gave them a list of all the offending websites. He asked them to watch out for any future nasty postings. He presented a list to parents of what they can do to prevent cyberbullying.

- Try to keep the home computer in a busy area of the house.
- Help your child set up online accounts including passwords and profiles. Keep personal information to an absolute minimum. Use a net nanny or parental control software.
- Review who you child is interacting with online; obtain a list.
- Know the latest acronyms and lingo use online.
- Discuss cyberbullying with your child. Make sure that you tell them that they will not be punished if they tell you they ae being cyberbullied.
- Tell your child not to respond to any cyberbully threats or comments online. Print them out and get help to verify and find the source. Pursue reporting the incidents to the service provider.
- Get the school involved in the process by reporting it and seeking regress or mediation.
- Any threats of physical harm must be reported to the police. Laws vary state to state.
- Be persistent and refuse to be discouraged by people failing to act or downplaying the incident

Sydney then traveled to the child's school to make sure they had a policy about cyberbullying and making sure they took appropriate action. They school did have a policy and explained it to Sydney.

SCHOOL BULLYING POLICY

- They taught children that it was okay to report abuse
- They had clear polices on cyberbullying.
- They made sure that they kept up with the latest online trends and social media sites.
- They educated all school personnel on cyberbullying and how to act.
- They had a program to get parents involved.
- They had open communication lines and outlets for children about cyberbullying.
- They taught the ethical use of computer technology.
- They collaborated with community and national resources on cyberbullying.
- Defined their zero-tolerance policy rules on cyberbullying.
- Had legal counsel and police resources available for advice.

Some of the cyberbullying postings were so bad or threatened harm so Sydney traveled to the police station and filed a police report on them.

Sydney discovered that each state has different laws on cyberbullying and how to file a police complaint.

Sydney then gathered up all of his friend monsters and went to a large computer presentation room. Sydney and his friend monsters made the all the girl's passwords, who had been cyber bullied, much stronger.

They did their best to block and prevent the cyber bullies from accessing any of her sites.

Next Sydney contacted all the cyber bully's parents and teachers and put them on notice about the cyber bullying and the actions that were taken and would be taken in the future, if the cyber bullying continued.

Then Sydney conducted a class with both children and parents together. He showed some of the mean postings to everyone. He asked the children to report mean postings to their parents and teachers. He urged parents to know and monitor their children's activities on the Internet, and to recognize some symptoms of cyber bullying like anger, depression and isolation.

The cyberbullies were required to go to a mandatory class on proper conduct on the internet and to participate in an anti-cyber bullying event.

Sydney gave them the names of some organizations who work to repair the damage of cyberbullying or prevent it.

The list is growing every day!

Sydney went on talk shows and gave seminars on stopping cyber bulling.

Sydney knew that he had done much good work stopping other bullies who bullied children in person. Sydney himself had been bullied by some other monsters because he was friendly with children and did not scare them.

He realized he had much more work to complete, especially with cyberbullies.

Sydney now rededicated himself to stopping cyber bullies. He became a force against cyber bullies.

Every day he searched the Internet for cyber bullies. He started a cyberbully help blog. He exposed cyber bullies for what they were, cowards. He made sure he educated more and more children, parents and teachers every day on what actions to take when they suffered from cyber bullying

ABOUT THE AUTHOR:

Dr. Tom DePaoli, is university professor, child advocate and consultant for his own company Apollo Solutions. Dr. Tom authored eight other books that are available on Amazon.com.
Dr. Tom can be contacted at his website http://www.apollosolutions.us or his email drtomd@gmail.com.

ABOUT THE ILLUSTRATOR

MISSION STATEMENT:
"Making the World A Happier Place, One Smile at a Time."™

"Art should be fun!" states illustrator Laurie Barrows. The artist's work sparkles with playfulness. Her positive approach to life shines through. Bright color celebrates the joy the artist finds in her subject. This is her 208th book.

"I carry my philosophy of life into my work. I believe in a positive attitude and the power of love," says Barrows, "My goal with children's art is to touch lives with the wonderful luxury of innocence by creating positive images for the young."

"Children need a positive and empowering environment in which to grow and flourish. Children need freedom to dream. Everyday should be a celebration of joy and wonder. Developing a sense of self through play fosters creativity, imagination, and problem solving. We can all benefit by returning to a simpler time, if only for a moment."

"Success has many definitions. If my work makes you smile, and brightens your day, I've been successful."

Made in the USA
Middletown, DE
12 April 2017